POEMS FROM LIMBO

BY THE SAME AUTHOR

Guitar
1951

Halcyon
1953

Mistral
1953

Lunar Corn
privately printed 1956

Poems from Limbo

ROB LYLE

STATE COLLEGE AT
FRAMINGHAM, MASSACHUSETTS

Dufour Editions

CHESTER SPRINGS

Heroic Elegies was published in a limited, signed
edition of 300 copies by The Hand and Flower
Press in 1957

DEDICATED TO
Anna

CONTENTS

Heroic Elegies

First Elegy

FOR ERICA MARX

The Gods have withdrawn to the mountain
Behind impenetrable mists that conceal their golden games
From abandoned incurious mortals,
And the golden light shines no more over the distance
Or in the uncomprehending bewildered eyes.

There is no possibility that the person one meets or passes
May be a divinity incarnate
One never born and never to be dead
Yet consorting with us because we have been inspired
And privileged to rub shoulders with Grace.

The skin of Marsyas hangs haggard from the leafless tree
And his flutes have been trampled into the ground.
From the mouth of the cave no sacred incense rises.
The glades are not disturbed by dances. From within the shrubbery
No sudden music trembles to enchant the heart.

Where are you, Gods, my God, serenest presences,
Image accompanying the morn the noon the eve
And moon of the mind's night?
Turning whatever corner of the garden
Once I was greeted by one aspect of you or another

But now I must seek you in darkness, remake you out of chaos,
Out of broken things, irretrievable years, sorrows, laughters,
Exiles and desires,
I must piece together again the fragments of your face and form
Obedient to the memory of my heart.

11

No longer able to pray each act becomes a prayer
And the act of creation is the act of love
The communion with a dream
Reality gazing at itself in a glass
The ear of the heart straining to catch the whisper of the Word.

But the danger is to make God into a statue
Or of a statue make a God. Only from Life comes life
And there is no beginning and no end.
Yet life is not life without its magic breath
And who can see a statue, without light?

I can create a city with wide boulevards, columns, colonnades,
Shady squares, spacious avenues, fountains, and solemn graves
Dark trees defining, and at its heart
A cold, smooth, empty dream of the divine
In whitest marble.

But I prefer from out this mortal state
To mirror mortal anguish. Desperate this must be
My answer to the Gods. I will create what they deny to us
And once more with my anguished love compel the myrtle,
Dance, and the sacrificial song.

Second Elegy

FOR MARGARET RUTHERFORD

It is my destiny to succumb to the temptation of Marsyas.
Who, dreaming of fame and lightly intoxicated,
Could turn away from those slender inviting reeds
That hold the secret of spontaneous song as through its rushes
Crystal the pure river untasted runs?

I am in love with music. Mysterious voices
Call me through pine and eucalyptus to the untrodden hill
Whither the Apollonian vision deigns to descend
Snow-footed, sandalled, dazzling winged,
Deigns to determine a contest whose issue is not in doubt.

Are we not instruments to be played and cast aside?
In my challenge is the certainty of defeat.
It is the divine duet which is my justification—
Counterpoint to creation making once
Let my remnants hang in the cave's mouth!

For we are always defeated before perfection
Or perfection being indivisible could not be,
But so long as I imperfect believe in perfection
Flute and tambourine must dance round my death
Celebrating one who has borne Truth tragic witness.

In my tribulation is my peace. Marsyas, had I not accepted your cloak
I too could be contented and comfortable. I know
Every poet who sets himself up against Apollo
Is doomed to be flayed alive and only avoids blasphemy
Being certain of guilt and certain of defeat.

13

Harp of Aeolus! Conch in whose memorial heart
Amphitrite sings! We too are shells, haphazard harps,
Full of wild echoes, whispers of Eden; hollows that are Earth's opened ears
Hearkening back into childhood when the friendly wind
Sang us to sleep in the familiar trees!

How should we move thus to our deaths but by that sound?
Migrating souls heavy-laden with remembered summers
Headed for shifting heavens full of light
We steer by instinctive long-forgotten stars
On stubborn calculating wings

Or following the wild sirens of the sea
Beyond the drifting halcyons, ocean-drowsy,
Are drawn to die in that wide, pleasant land
Among the welcoming and well-known voices.
So, let me take you up

Incomparable flutes! You fill me with the love
That inspiration must equate with Providence
And so would perish to preserve.
Blow amorous winds across my pine-hung heart,
Draw from my madness or my death such sweeping harmonies

As shall both testify to Marsyas' martyrdom
And urge through some young ear in this lost time
A leaping soul to lean from all but love
And to the hills returning
Prove worthy of the Apollonian ire!

Third Elegy

FOR MIRANDA LYLE

They will not listen.
They do not want to hear, it makes them uncomfortable.
They have no means of knowing what it is all about
And if they did they would not like it.
Don't attempt to engage their attention.

Though every Spring, in the Algarve, the almond blossoms,
The songs have migrated, winged, following another Sun.
When the chill comes they foregather and prepare for flight.
Restlessly they turn and wheel, hither and thither,
Forewarned of the coming of the killing cold.

This is no time for tears. The long wake
Has ended in exhaustion and drunken sleep.
The wind blows through the deserted square lifting the cloths from the café tables.
It is time to drain the last glass, gather together pens, notebooks, papers.
It is time to pack up and depart.

But first, a few duties to be performed.
Settle all debts, resolve all quarrels, forgive enemies and friends.
Leave behind neither want, heartache, nor bitterness.
Destroy all that is trivial or unworthy.
In mind and body it is necessary to travel light.

Above all, think deeply on death. This is no matter to be left to others.
The long planks of cypress must be ordered and cut and polished.
Provision must be made against that last enormous day.
Heroes, without giving too much trouble to others,
Let us depart in style, fastidiously, and with due respect for the Future!

15

In the distance the mountain calls with perpetual summer snow
Beyond the hangover hives, beyond the gymnastic beaches,
Beyond the stucco'd villas' grinning masks
There, where, still, the exiled Gods hold converse,
Trailing their fingers in the waters of Aganippe!

The greatest grief is not to die at home,
Is not to say farewell in the grand manner.
The deepest sadness is to die alone.
Yet every day that is lived in love is a day of death.
We die a thousand deaths before we die and, by rehearsal, learn to go.

Only those who are alive think about death.
The dead think of nothing but life and of how important it is.
Only the impotent are obsessed by sex.
But the Gods dwell beyond the confines of life
In the interior deep glades of death.

We should visit the cemeteries to pay our respects to the dead.
It is only right and proper.
But one does not camp there, build a house, or set up shop.
That would be blasphemous, an insult to the dead
Who are the only living.

No, afterwards, with due decorum, and a few appropriate prayers
For the repose of the souls of the dead,
We depart for the ruthless light and the anguish of the white road,
Although for a long time still
Lies on our spirits the shade of the shrouding cypress.

It was momentarily a great temptation perhaps to yield down there to sleep,
Relinquishing all cares. For a time it is restful to conform
And cease from thought. But come, we must shake ourselves free,
For we seek a different death, a clamour full of strange cries
And murmurous with immortal moments.

16

Fourth Elegy

FOR ELIZABETH LYON

Let us not imagine that we can cultivate our garden of maimed statues
Behind a high wall sprinkled with broken glass!
Let us not deceive ourselves.
Every reporter carries a rope-ladder in his pocket
And his nose is as long as the night.

Let us rather make everything ready. Simplicity is essential
And continual neatness. We must decide now what we need
Which is to say, how much we can leave behind.
So little is really necessary and in the hour of parting
Love will resolve the mind's paralysis.

We face a long journey. The way is hard and the end uncertain.
We shall certainly be tempted to turn back to the peace of our secret seclusion
Who can never be rid of the past.
We have not even had time for the needful training,
Rigorous disciplines, forced marches, deprivations.

Perhaps it is already too late. I have seen the pale-faced heralds
Stumbling, exhausted, into the city from behind the mountains,
With swollen tongues. But they have no need of speech.
Already the smoke of fires rises into the dark dawn
And the wind stinks of sacrifice.

But we are also besieged from within and are liable to be tried as traitors
Or, more probably, stoned. The slow attrition by those who have no will to survive
Is more terrible than the assault of hostile warriors.
Yet even in winter we must not despair of crossing the mountains
Or reaching the region where burns the sacred fire.

A*   17

My people: it is our misfortune that we cannot wholly reject you
In token of which we abandon to your blind irreverence
The husbandry of years. Indeed, we are almost grateful
To discover how little was really essential
And how much was merely habit.

Now, as we leave, at the source of our immense solitude
Compassion is born for the wingless and born-to-be-conquered,
Our wrath is turned rather against the seers and savants,
Against those who have perverted the omnipotent Word
And poisoned the waters of crystal.

Come now, dawn is breaking behind the hills.
Let us pass swiftly out of the sleeping city.
How many leagues, how many years, without maps, under what obscure stars!
But at least there will be no deceptions, no lies,
And, above all, no newspapers.

Now, here, from the final meadows, let us draw breath and look back
Upon all we have had to abandon. The graceful house
With its windows full of the dawn. The long lawns and the silent cedars.
The orchards, drooping with abundance. The vines
Turning to red and purple and gold.

The farm-buildings with their quiet stalls. The armoury
Containing our bows of seasoned yew and horn, and the well-matched,
        whispering arrows.
The statues white in the waking glades, bird-song, the butterfly meads, and
        beyond
The unfolding, close-cropped, delicate sheep-pastures—
O! Why are we not also with our shepherds?

Fifth Elegy

FOR DOMINIC LYLE

It is time to be going, for there is no doubt that night is waning,
That the stars have gone on ahead, and dawn is near.
Already the watch has twice been changed: one only remains.
Spartans, it is time to gird on our armour and put a comb through our hair.
And may we not pass away piteously in the flower.

Now is the time to recollect ancient disciplines;
To put all to the test. We alone are conscious of our destiny.
On either flank slumber allies in whom we may put no trust.
Behind us the sleepless sea by which way is no retreat,
And before us probable death, but also fame undying.

At this hour it is appropriate to pay homage to the Gods whom we seek.
Let each one therefore pray and propitiate as he has been taught,
Some with penance, some with wide-horned oxen, others with white barley,
And all with a generous libation of precious wine.
And may our single prayer rise to heaven with the smoke from our fires.

It is right, too, to remember the broad acres of home,
Dwelling each of us for a moment on his wife, sweetheart, or children,
On the work of our hands, on our relinquished possessions,
On our fathers whose blood we are determined not to dishonour,
On our native fields whose wheat we reap in our bones though far from home.

Happy is he whom his own earth holds fast in fatal peace,
Lying unforgotten and visited
By children and friends in the solicitous shifting shade
Under the grass that wanders with the grazing wind
That once through a boy's hair played as rill through reeds.

Happy is he whom his loved Lakedaimon calls
At the last, out of the past, across immeasurable wept seas'
Breaking years to think of home
And wound in his own wounds
Fall dreaming of different trees and his unforgettable fields.

Happy is he whom the haunting delirious foam
Deceives to dream of a Thessaly's drumming hooves
Or through the flap of his tent see only Argive pastures
Perfumed with memories, lit with unspeakable longings,
And purified by doom.

Happy is he whom Phrygian vineyards fill
With far-off fragrance, in his last lanced hour recalls
His secret Pteleos deep in meads;
Who, lying quiet among holy haphazard stones
Rests fruitful and unashamed, his conscience clear.

Happy is he whose sons remember him
Him whose loins gave birth long ago to a lovelier star
Over barbarian battlements burning a Hector heart
Guiding the lost life back to the scattered straw's
Grave cradle of death's immaculate desire!

But perhaps such is not our lot. We may not outstare the blue nor interpret the
        stars by daylight,
But turning within may possibly dream the inscrutable.
So, having given due time and regard to the soul's imperious obligations
Let us still the heart's anguish with deeper, deepest desire:
For the morning calls, and the fateful fight, and the claims of manhood.

Sixth Elegy

FOR HUGH LYLE

Our place is by the gate, in the deep-shade of the oak-tree,
The high wall rising behind, and within, the sacred fire
Under cloudy towers. Our triumph is certain; our defeat
Only another triumph. See, now, how through the leaves
The sun's caressing fingers fondle bronze!

We have need of armour of the finest quality, well beaten; shields
Exquisitely embossed; swords cavern-tempered; lithe spears of finest ash;
Of whispering arrows tipped with obsidian
And curly bows horn-capped. And from our brows let nod
Contemptuous plumes; thus shall our dust be golden!

And in our hearts may anguish conceive fruitfully
Blood-firing, comradely, campaigning song,
Deep song of the remorseless blood till, in the pass
We stand, as once before we stood, under treacherous cliffs
And sell our lives for letters, carved in stone.

In our hearts also love, as we would have love always
With shining shield to deflect the inevitable spear
Of avaricious envious hate. For we would wear
Our love like hatred overcome by tears
Wedding our woes to war.

I have found it hard to forgive Achilles his treatment of Hector's body,
But we, my friends, are going to be treated with even less ceremony.
Yet I can see why the wrath of Achilles remained implacable—
That his hatred of Hector mirrored his love for Patroklos—
For in battle a friend is irreplaceable.

21

There must be someone with whom we may speak without misunderstanding.
Though we commune with God, we yet are men;
And of what use is it to speak with God if we cannot speak with each other?
Therefore in my heart I forgive Achilles because of his love
And may our courage equal our love in the hour of decision also!

True, we appear betrayed; have the Gods abandoned us?
No, not even divine decree can sever us from mankind.
Their fault is ours and we bear it into battle.
Each one of us can hang, if only momentarily, from the torturing tree.
And it befits us, my heroes, to suffer, as we think, unjustly.

What is the war about? A woman's beauty? One
Most like unto the immortal goddesses to look upon?
Something for which no common man would fight
Except for gold, or to escape from his job or his wife?
No, but immeasurable disaster, the being made blind with the blind.

What great consolation shall our still-ringing armour
Give to the pitifully vanquished in the days to come!
Woe to the victors!
As through their fingers trickles our bloody dust!
As with mouths bitter with ashes they call us back by name!

Hence these preparations. And while we await the onslaught
Let us remember the weak, the destitute, and the sorrowful.
And there are always the sick and the hurt to be tended.
Let us give what strength and comfort we can where most they are needed.
There is nothing else to be done.

Seventh Elegy

FOR MARGARET RAWLINGS

Victory and defeat alike are in the hands of God
Who alone can distinguish between them
As indeed we acknowledge when we act as Gods
But pray as men. And are they prayers—these silent exhalations
Supplicating victories that will be defeats?

The victory which I had always envisaged is impossible,
And I have come to believe that it would also be undesirable.
What use have we for power, riches or renown?
But from over the twilight river I see a brother beckoning
And with brimming heart I raise my arm in salute!

The world's divisions are arbitrary and we hold them in contempt
Or all is lost; for we are weak to the world.
I acknowledge only the light of recognition across rooms full of people,
Over streets, over cities, across frontiers and fields of battle,
The light brighter than banners for which we are as badly-tended lamps

Whence alone is victory and the defeat of Fate.
For even as the leaves—quivering glory and consolation of Summer—
Turn at last, and wither, and are carried away by the wind—
Until a new Spring brings to birth a new foliage—
Even so are the generations of men.

But I am interested only in immortality,
In the unquenchable green flame of the leafy generations
Changeless behind change, in the winged soul that escapes from the wound
To what fantastic flights! I have heard the voice of a brother calling with a
     thousand echoes
In the hollow heart, as in thick-leaved Thisbe, that haunt of doves.

And who is my brother? Only he
To whom I might be a brother also.
I am an army in myself and must
Die many deaths, submit to many sieges, be tempted, time and again, to have
      recourse to the long ships:
And my soul is swarming with spies.

Before contending hosts we elect for single combat,
Battling to overcome our unruly selves
That thus the scales of destiny may be dipped in our favour
And I am closer to my elect opponent
Than to the anonymous hordes at my back.

Only in divining the Will of the Gods,
Only by inspired anticipation,
Only by submission to what is truly creative
Shall we avoid the fate of the numberless destined
To be crushed at the meeting of hosts.

We have need of a deeper communion and will find one another
Only after heroic separations.
Thus alone can we know each other, maintaining contact
As by the winding of a horn overhead in the heart,
Even as still there sounds down deep gorges

And over the estranging mountain
Roland's desperate, heroic call.
And thinking on these things I looked up and beheld the coming of Autumn,
Gathering clouds, rain-bearing gusts, and a sky
Full of wild birds. An evil omen.

Eighth Elegy

FOR TERESA CUSTODIO

You who have experienced love and in the face of infinite bitterness have not
    rejected it:
You who know that love moves the sun and the other stars
Even to the farthest conflagrations: You who live by love
No matter with what anguish or even in despair:
Listen to me!

There is no victory but only the defeat of Fate.
There are no victors but only those who are free from Fate.
For Fate breeds Anguish, Anguish terrible cry of the soul caught in the vice
    of Fate,
Anguish the ultimate discord of inherited agony
Demanding resolution.

In moments of despair it is helpful to go to the keyboard
And sound the full chord of C major. Freed by the sustaining pedal
The strings with a thousand echoes and reverberations
Will continue to tremble with this sublime Chord,
Purest and most monumental of harmonies,

Evoking as it were in a dark vault
A thousand sympathetic voices, the quiet amens
Of the under and overtones, the descant of angelic harmonics,
And the mysterious vibrations of the inaudible sounds, which, dying away into
    the illimitable distance,
Will fade as when a heavenly portal closes.

25

Such is resolution, the floating whitest marble
On which the writhing-in-death discord comes to rest;
The perfect proportion and harmony of Peace.
And this most sweet serene concordance is basically a simple triad
Composed of three equal and mutually necessary notes.

In this one chord it is possible to see with Ignatius Loyola
Reflected as in a pool the image of the Trinity.
The tonic is God the Father, the dominant God the Son, and the lovely sub-
          mediant
Is the love between them, completing and joining,
White-winged, the Holy Ghost.

Thus, as even in the most tortured dissonance
Is predicated the peace of an ultimate resolution
In which the clashing conflicting parts find restful harmony
And mutual love and perfect understanding, so in our tragic situation
Is predicated the possibility of freedom.

Now Anguish is as necessary to the life of the soul
As is pain to the life of the body. Hence, now, the Hero
Hearing continually the strident discord of Fate
And piteously conscious of the tonic solution
Yet powerless to bring it about.

This is our stage, one free of all superfluities.
The background bare, black velvet,
The Furies hissing from the wings and the masked Hero
Alone among myrmidons, in his perpetually self-imposed anguish the promise
Of the possible resolution, our redemption.

26

For the Hero embraces Anguish in order to live,
In order not to be wholly enslaved by Fate;
And in his heroism asserts our last hope and our only Freedom
Who holds in his martyred heart the truth of the common chord:
The Triad nailed to the towering three-pronged Tree.

Ninth Elegy

FOR TONY AND URSULA VAN DEN BURGH

"With the putting on of the tragic mask,
With the assumption of the mantle of tragedy,
With the raising of the curtain upon the last and greatest of all stages,
In the wind that blows perpetually from the wings,
I am here to expiate the dreams of generations.

I come of a doomed line. Terrible disasters,
Crimes and catastrophes, are latent in my blood.
And possible madness. And I doubt if in days to come
A grocer's assistant of genius
Will be able to predict the exact location of my tomb.

I desire to speak for the speechless. My head rings with the clamour of crowds.
I am a character in search of an author.
Your speech is not my speech, yet I understand you.
Your ways are not my ways, yet I am bound to you.
Poets, where are the lines of which I can only dream?

In my heart the thought-to-be-born cries for deliverance.
But, alas, nothing can exist until it is named;
Its existence remains potential.
Even so the concept of an irresistible sword
May languish for years, wanting its unmined metal.

Believe me, I am bound to you because I cannot escape;
But you, equally, are bound to me.
We share the same contaminated blood.
Nightly the Furies peck at the windows of both our houses
And in the morning they pursue us without distinction.

All the same, I have been sorely tempted to yield to Fate!
Is there a lover in the world who has not sometimes dreamed
Of the joys of a leisurely, heart-free existence?
And yet, though on the whole vegetables lead careless, happy lives,
They are destined to be eaten.

Fate is only intolerable so long as we are not resigned to it,
But you, you have made your pact with Fate
And then, of course, Fate becomes wonderfully accommodating!
And I too have been tempted to make friends with Fate,
To relinquish the unequal struggle.

Nothing is easier than to love a conquered enemy!
His very existence is essential to the conqueror's pride.
That is why Fate seems to favour you, you have made your submission—
But is there not still in your heart, in your blood,
Disturbing, a cell, a bacillus of guilt?

Do you not hear, sometimes, in your unguarded moments
The cry of my Anguish, as it were a familiar voice that summons you out of
       sleep,
A voice not born of dreams but apparently real and manifest
So that you are awake in an instant and go to the window and search the
       uttermost darkness
For someone who cannot be there?

Such is my voice, the voice of one who like some Wandering Jew
Walks through the world out of Time, full of weariness, listening for the
       lost words.
I have had visions because I remember
Where you forget. The curse of memory is also the curse of prophecy.
And, I have seen the gallows green with leaves."

Tenth Elegy

FOR PETER GRANVILLE FELL

Now in the Hero's stuttering speech is heard
The cry of the reborn Marsyas, presumptuous still
In the shreds of a blind beggar challenging the aloof Apollo;
The sigh of the Black Knight wandering the wet woods,
The ache of the heart remembering antique voices.

For Marsyas has broken from the thicket with the ageless cry of the Spring
And the rider has raised his chin long sunk on his breast to listen—
In the haggard eyes under the vizor the first light of recognition
(Though ever the mailed hands clutch at the skull's smooth sockets)
That the wintry pilgrimage is coming at last to an end.

And the dog cocks his ears and points, and the flitting shrouded shadow
Stays in the trees as a figure drags itself down to the river,
To the creaking virginal reeds,
Leaving on the leaves a speckled, wounded trail, first flower
Of the long-congealed new-budding blood's green wine.

Let him drink long and deep of the fresh, cold, bearded water.
He has come far, on foot, across the most distant mountains.
Rain, wind, sun! Time has grizzled him, his old wounds ache.
Yet, soon he will stand, and walk, and with dark eyes abstracted,
Frame his lips to the music that now he remembers with wonder.

And the Knight who has seen his shadow stretched by a shattered sun
To blanket the world, will know his exile ending,
His vigilant patience rewarded. However, he will not hope, nor sip at the
    dews of dream
But will be as one long bent who, reading between the clouds,
Predicts without pride the motions of the elemental Will.

He will rather persist in his way because there is no other;
Because, after all, by virtue of his astounding vision
Of the Marsyas martyred remade in the snowdrift womb of the world
Surviving the flood and the cold and the solar sorrow
He has not endured in vain the companionship of his horrible escorts.

For, as from the bare bombed site sprouts the long-buried corn,
As from the furtive plague-pit blooms the grass so green,
As from the obliterating volley the victor's smile is born,
As from the battlefield, jasmine-crucified, amaranth spurts,
As from the grave the lily like a breast,

So in his soul is born not hope but the unsought solace
Of loosened streams in earth's cold veins in the mushroom dawn,
The joyful bleak blind cry of birth in the forked wastes of pain,
The anguished lament of love, condemned to re-enter the world—
Love, whose piteous wail is a shuddering spasm of praise!

And a great weeping exultation sweeps his heart!
Even as through the shivering forests awakened dripping with thaw
The suddenly warm wind winds until the giants
Dissolve in gusty tears, shaken by sobs—
Even so does he know in his heart, desire, the dead, arisen.

Yet nothing is changed. With Death and his own shadow still at his side
He must ride on. Yet all is transformed; because now his relentless way
That was a numb, dull, armoured act of the Will,
Is crossed by the truth, sly as the early fox, that desire is deathless
And nurtures resurrections in its wounds.

CASCAIS, PORTUGAL, 25th September, 1956.

31

NOTES

FOURTH ELEGY

LINE 50   cf. *Ah perché non son io co' miei pastori?* Gabriele d'Annunzio, *I Pastori*, from *Alcyone*.

FIFTH ELEGY

The first three lines are a paraphrase of a passage in the *Iliad*.

SIXTH ELEGY

v. 8, LINE 2 cf. *Iliad*, Bk. III, lines 154–158.

SEVENTH ELEGY

v. 4, LINES 2–5 cf. *Iliad*, Bk. VI, lines 146–149.

EIGHTH ELEGY

LINE 2 cf. *L'amor che muove il sole e l'altre stelle* Dante, *Paradiso*.

Interval

Reflets dans l'Eau

(PORTINHO DA ARRABIDA)

The white beach is bruised with purple sea-urchins washed up by the tide
High up on the cliffs birds are wheeling slowly as lazy thoughts
On a hillock of white sand a single stunted pine-tree stands like a stork in its
    pool of shade
A young man stripped to the waist rides by on a black horse
He rides it into the sea that is the colour of a tree full of parrots
Far out on the sandbank the surf breaks with the sound of blood in a deep conch
In the harbour prows graceful as a swan's breast lie at anchor, phoenician
    sandals discarded on a mosaic floor
Indolently over the bay pass torsos of salted copper swaying to the single oar
Under the thin water my feet are white as the feet of a corpse.

Regret

Long shadows dimming the young lawns
In slow dark waves as suns go down
Suck at my heart

Pure voices in the orchards of the past
(When streams ran clear in the appled Autumn
And the shade was innocent)

Ring bells of flowers dim as falling dew.
And the nights of careless sleep
White as childhood

Soft cobwebs of the moon on field and tree
Capture my flying dreams
And again I remember

How little time they have to live like that
Giving me back my lost years—
And that we are divided.

The Morning Watch

I awoke before dawn,
Restless, disturbed by dreams,
And, at first light, I climbed
With the help of my sticks
As so often before
The steep steps to the tower

And when I arrived in the open air
Dawn was breaking.
Receding mists revealed
Lakes, opening eyes.
Darkness gave birth
To distant hills
And down the white road
The young day cantered.

Road that winds to fade beyond the hill,
Will you bring me my heart's desire this morning?

With straining eyes
Eager as the rising sun
I waited for the plume of dust
For the plume on his helmet
For the flash of his harness
Who, so long ago,
Had gone away.

Would he recognize me?
Would my features be familiar?
Would he smile, or frown?

The sun rose and the earth
Smiled out of sleep.
How clear the hills, the wide far distance, the plain,
the trees, the pristine road of dreams!

And Oh, again, again,
Only the empty sky,
The empty road,
And the empty heart.

Flight 152

With a wave of your sad hand you dismissed me
From your too intimate pain to go back
Into the crowd, into the eyeless anonymity
That covers parting, heartache, and utter lack.

O yes, I'd stood elect in a unique morning,
Singled out by your smile, by your embrace
Called to a sudden and mysterious adorning
Of a self with changed heart and a changed face.

But now, the sky's claimed you again, the southern noon
Will welcome you down, and the wistful leaf;
While I—I'll step over staring multitudes, alone
On the equivocal tightrope of grief.

Roy Campbell

He was larger than those around him and walked uneasily
    Among the puny and mediocre in an unheroic age.
'There were giants in those days'—and he was one of them,
    A last survivor, putting us to shame with a reminder
Of antique simplicity and ancient greatness. In him
    The emotions were undiluted and stripped of accretions expressed
An original purity. He was Odysseus, wise in counsel,
    Ever mindful of his Penelope and his home; ever sustained
By heroic patience, giant Will, and not a little
    Subtlety and cunning; one who had heard with unstopped ears
The Sirens' song, and lived; one in whom courage and resource
    Were never wanting. He ever stood free and erect
In defiance of Fortune. His huge frame
    Could have strung and drawn with ease the fabulous bow, his anger
Appalled effete and cringing suitors. His wide and maritime eyes
    Volatile as the chromatic sea seemed ever to gaze
Beyond the Pillars out towards unknown exploits. He was, above all,
    As befits one of heroic stature, kind and gentle; full of rich song
And delighted laughter; gay courtesy and splendid gesture.
    Great drinker; inexhaustible lover; warrior and witness of Truth
      whom the Gods loved

Africa gave him life, Lusitania death. He lies
    In Southern hills, poet of shepherds, herdsmen, winds and waters.

Envoi

I am not one who proceeds by mystic leaps.
These I have essayed, and fallen. No,
I am of those to whom Wisdom comes
Full of mistrust, on hesitating feet.

In an age when poets outnumber priests, I, a poet,
Am appalled by the popularity of poetry, that science of solitude.
The slopes of Helicon are strewn with polished bones:
The pubs and cafés are filled with those who have turned back.

Even as I write, I am aware of the terrible egotism
That threatens myself, my love, and all my own.
Things change at dawn; doubt comes; then, for an hour or two,
Abandoned by black-sandalled sleep, we know the Hell
Our Heaven predicates: or, even in the midst of our so-wrapt embrace,
Suffer that pang among the flowers,
Delight's own bitterness, and its confirmation.

Is there a deeper death than Winter to the world?
This is the dark side of the moon, the werewolf's anguish.
Who can bear this solitude, this aridity?

This is a thought that becomes all the more terrible
When I contemplate the fragility of fame;
When I consider that all my admiration of the good and the beautiful
Has made me neither good nor beautiful;
That I have committed too many, irremediable sins,
And have even, perhaps, persevered in error;
That I have nothing to put in the scales on the other side
But an abandoned heart, and a handful of imperfect verses.
Do you wonder then, that I grow irresolute,
Appalled by the perfection required of a poet?

Orphic Elegies

TO MY MOTHER

First Elegy

FOR DEBORAH CHATTAWAY

I have seen Babel building: I have witnessed
The confusion of tongues. Where is it now,
The song in the flowers name
At the sound of which it trembles? Lost harmonies!
The glass does not sing, but breaks. Jericho's down.
Now brother may not speak with brother,
Where there is knowledge but no understanding.

Therefore I do not speak in words but in rumours.
High in the azure I strike the note of the Sun:
High where the Prince in red and gold on an ice-white horse
Rides by the dry tree:
So far, so high, only the ear of desire
(The exile's ear) remembering, can hear,
So that he weeps, babbling the lovely name.

But immediately I must go down, turning my back on the lover
Whose heart bleeds like Autumn over the withering grass.
I must go down in search of the precious waters,
And carry them back to the world, and lead them
Over the channelled and terraced fields
To nurture the Green Ear of Wheat.
And give us this day our supersubstantial bread.

I can't go on. I don't want to continue
To add to the pain in the world.
I have worked long hours, day after day,
And often far into the night:
And I was blind, because I was successful.
I have been honoured, rewarded, acclaimed, for my rate of production.
I might even have been made a foreman.

But now I have given in my notice. I have turned away
From he who was: I am alone and I am bewildered.
I have turned away from the benches where pain is made,
For I do not want to go on
Adding to the pain in the world.
I have struck the highest note, the note of the Sun, I want to hear
Only the song that passes up to Heaven.

Give us this day the gift of tears. I want to weep.
I'm tired of the arid and arrogant heart,
Of the frozen eyes. I want to know who I am
(If there's anyone there to know) I want to be
Led by the hand, away from this ludicrous grief.
I want light, ever more light, the Sun to burn and leave
Only a broken and a contrite heart.

You who have turned from the City's teeming ruins
And the shrill voices of Babel's men and women
Talking of politics and sex,
You know the sudden silence and the anguished joy
In the awful shadow cast by the dead metropolis,
And how we long to turn back, and hesitate, and hear
Music on the unbelievably undarkened hill.

Second Elegy

FOR HUGH OLOFF DE WET

Can you see the almond from the window of your cell?
Have you observed that each year, briefly,
It burns with translucent fire,
And that we haven't much time?
But then, it is almost all that happens! And after,
Do you still consider the walls insurmountable?
Or have you, perhaps, contemplated escape?

From the dark tower the watchman cried night and morning.
On Sundays the bells ring.
The gruel is thin and the bread bitter.
But, even so, it would seem to be safer inside.
The light is blinding, it burns the eyes.
And did you really see the almond in flower,
Or was it only imagination?

Yet what if on a sigh of wings the Angel
With his echoing voice that sounds only in the mind
Appeared to you and announced that you were free
And you saw that your shackles had never been locked
And your cell-door never fastened?
Would you rise then with closed eyes and hesitating steps,
Or cower back into the remotest corner?

It is possible to shut out the light:
It is possible to live in darkness:
It is possible to die, and not be dead.
The dead do not know each other; shade denies shade.
In the gloom there is no recognition:
In the cold there is only violence and regret:
In the night there is no choice at all

But to live blindly in the enormous fatigue of Time,
In the dense darkness that is under the world:
In the chaos where even a glimmer of light
Is unbearable; where everything must begin all over again
From the beginning. Teach us to bear the light!
Teach us to bear the last light without fainting!
Pray for us sinners, now and *at the hour of our death.*

Yet, do I want to know that I am at liberty?
Do I want to go out by the open door
And shoulder suffering like a wounded comrade?
It is so haunting, so sad, so harsh, so unfamiliar!
Out there, every movement is awkward and painful:
I've grown so used to the uniform, to the prison fare,
I am sucked back into my past as into a quicksand.

But I have seen the almond from the window of my cell.
I cannot rest or be content any longer.
Now, in the sleepless hours, reluctant as a shadow on a field
Will deepest sorrow steal over my heart,
Recalling in anguish the done and the undone,
And opening my eyes to the wounding words of the Angel:
Light, agonizing Light, and Memory Eternal!

Third Elegy

FOR ROBIN HAYTER

The delicate musician who is not afraid of death
Is able to defeat the most redoubtable swordsman:
Even so did the gentle Teamaster
Conquer the bully by the pond of Shinobazu.
The only problem is to become invulnerable;
For the true warrior is without violence,
And luminous in the armour of understanding.

And the true warrior, who is without violence,
He in whom the sword and the will are as one
Has been tempered in long and exhausting battles:
He has conquered himself, he has set himself free
From the compulsion that binds all creatures until,
Wrapped in his cloak, at first light, awaiting attack,
His whole attention is given to the wild cyclamen.

But do *I* dare to look in that solar shield
And see my Self? Shall I not ask you then to pity me
And share my suffering? We would be turned to stone!
The snakes would no longer hiss, they would be suddenly still.
My own image! That is a fury I dare not face.
Yet, should some Archimedean Perseus come, and hold
His mirror to the world, would we not freeze, marbled with horror?

But the world will not help me, for I am the world.
I did what I condemn; I judged, and hanged my self.
I wept over fallen roses, and my tears
Watered thorns and nettles and briars.
I murdered my brother in my heart, calling him Cain.
How can I look? I don't want to look! Now I know
Why Lucifer has such hopeless eyes!

Even a glimpse is enough. I would never have left had I not suddenly seen
An image that repelled me, until I exclaimed:
'No, this is not I—that is not what I am!'
And now I am lonely and uncomfortable:
I understand why I am not good to live with.
But here, in the silence, I'm exposed to the awful voice:
Du sollst der werden, der du bist.

It occurs to me to pray. But to whom should I pray?
There is no one left whom I haven't offended.
It would be easier to go back, to forget.
But even there, eventually, it will strike midnight at the Ball
And the hour will come for the stripping of the masks
When all will stand still, and aghast.
And there shall be wailing and gnashing of teeth.

Then when the clock strikes and we see ourselves as we really are,
It will be of no avail to have run away to the Moon,
Or danced through the light-years in the great Spiral of Space
Down Time's inverted telescope to the snuffed-out end.
But in my mind, as memory, is the Book of Judgement:
I can look now, and understand, and I may see
That the awful Cloud is suddenly full of birds.

Fourth Elegy

FOR CRISTINA LYLE

Between the whirl of the waters
And the whirl of the wind; in the whirling ecstasy
I seek the calm at the heart of the hurricane:
Between the violence of murder
And the violence of suicide
(Between one sleep and another)
I seek the moment of consciousness, the Golden Mean.

The power of the atom is the left hand of the power of numbers.
The one leads down to the farthest dark, to the cold,
To the Region of Chaos:
And the other rises from note to note
Into the Heaven that is above the Heavens.
On the one hand there is Scientific Knowledge,
And on the other, the Laws of the Tetrachtys.

Who now may summon the white tiger of the West
And curb ill-tempered ministers, in the autumn season?
Or bend the people, as spring winds the grass,
By sounding the blue dragon of the eastern sea?
Who now will unify the intervals
Or bring to birth the celestial *symphonia*?
Each aeon the scale begins on a lower note.

51

The passionate activity that leads only to violence,
The idealisms that are only dreams,
All this *doing* that is merely twitching,
Are the results of false correspondences.
The lyra of Hermes has long been disrupted.
Things are no longer arranged in a certain order,
In that form by which the Cosmos resembles God.

'If the tonic be disturbed, the Prince is arrogant.
If the supertonic be disturbed, there is corruption.
If the mediant be disturbed, the people suffer.
If the dominant be disturbed, there is complaint.
If the submediant be disturbed, resources are lacking.
If all Five be disturbed, then there is IMPUDENCE:
The destruction of the Kingdom may come in less than a day. . . .

'In periods of chaos the modes are corrupted;
Sorrow is without dignity, and joy is not serene.
The music of opposition is indecent.
But when there is harmony there is no admixture;
Adultery is unknown, the Eyes are radiant;
The Liver and the Blood are clear and balanced;
Habits are in harmony, and there is peace.'

For each thing has its sound, which is its life—
The wood anemone, the flint, the seventh wave,
The bone, the bamboo shoot, the sole Arabian tree,
The lynx, and the lonely heart. This Amphion knew
When Thebes rose wondering as he fingered the five strings.
And we? Are we too late to be awed by *La novita del suono*,
To faint with desire to know the heavenly cause?

Fifth Elegy

FOR LIZA HARLAND

It is necessary to contemplate the sorrow of a God
Who cannot deprive us of the possibility of suicide:
For all of these notes have been sounded from the beginning,
Even as Mozart heard the Jupiter in an instant of time—
And how could he conceivably interfere?
If he had interfered we would never have heard of him:
Everything would have been different.

But we are created in the image of God
And are microcosmic in the Creation
(And the Ten Thousand Things are One)
Therefore of what use is it to panic outward to the stars
When we contain the farthest stars and the Earth and the Moon,
Saturn's rings and the Galaxy and the Sun?
Yet, in our hearts, God is sorrowful.

I know He exists because I have heard Him weeping.
In my heart, for a moment, I've been introduced to the Sorrow of God
Over an experiment that has failed.
And I also have wept because of that failure;
Because it is I who have failed.
Why then should we hope in the shadow of those wings?
No, I can't bear to contemplate the Agony of God.

We know of Him only because of our sorrow,
The sorrow that cannot be faced because it is real.
There is nothing real in us that is not of God:
There is nothing real in us that is not anguish:
Our anguish is holy.
And the rest is hostile, and determined to conquer.
All iniquity will pass away when I am no longer iniquitous.

All the wars of the world are as nothing to this war;
They are only the fruits of iniquity.
We, we are all Armageddons, but the others
Are only playgrounds
Where children mimic their elders, and wonder why.
And how can I expect statesmen to be other than ridiculous
When I myself do not dare to contemplate what I have done?

Don't speak to me of miracles; there is only more or less understanding;
And we pay for understanding by beating our breasts.
But we want to be comfortable, do we not?
So it's better to sleep, but of course without dreaming—
For who wants to wake up at three in the morning
Or give up drinking to be tortured by remorse?
It is easy to love one's neighbour when he is happy.

Therefore it is simpler to deny God,
For no child likes to see his father crying
('Really, you might control yourself in front of the children!')
There are so many ways of keeping oneself asleep,
It's no trouble to forget one is made in the image of God—
And, after all, you have led a good life and done what you could!
No, I don't want to see His Face streaming with tears.

Sixth Elegy

FOR ROLLO AND JEANNE GAMBLE

On this vast stage whose perspectives are lost in silence
The actors are numerous as the leaves of the forest,
As the generations of men.
Among waterfalls and rocks, in lamp-lit alleys,
Amid the gaunt facsimiles of factories,
In drawing-rooms and bedrooms of two dimensions,
We play our parts, improvising a lost drama.

Here there is no respect for the Unities.
We seem intent to play all the scenes simultaneously.
The prompter (is there a prompter?) cannot be heard above the din.
A wind blows perpetually from the wings.
Our eyes are red with dust and weeping.
We are characters in search of an Author:
Hysteric mimes, burlesques, *hypokritoi* . . .

And Solon rebuked Thespis . . .
And their wounds are real as the wounds of Peisistratus,
Where every tenement is a house of Atreus,
Where Clytemnestras of the suburbs beat crimson carpets,
Where Orestes lounges against the wall with a fag drooping from his lips,
Where down in the basement his red-clawed sister sulks through a
        novelette . . .
Can it be that *they do not know?*

Whose are the words? No one knows: it's a lost play.
Are they improvising, or quarrelling over the text?
Impossible to say. And what is going on over there?
It's too dark to see. It could be . . . Oh, anything can happen!
But the director? The producer? The carpenter?
And the electricians? On the stage. All on the stage.
They have joined in. They're all in it now.

He who appears idle is contemplating violence.
She who is still is recovering from violence.
Here and there, screams of pain:
Inquisitors in immaculate overalls.
In the darkness red flares of anger, living snarls.
A girl in tears, leaning over the rail of a liner.
Partings, separations, lies, and always, hunger.

Affairs of state for which masks are obligatory:
Politicians with the heads of cockatoos:
Scenes of famine, bodies countless as ears of corn:
Bloodshed, exquisite eruptions, disintegrating scenery:
Children crying, lovers devouring each others hearts:
And, amid scenes of rape and hysteria,
An artist, meticulously painting an apple.

Why, when we forgot our parts, when we no longer understood,
Did we not fall silent? What happened? What went wrong?
For we are actors no longer; we're not acting any more.
There isn't even an audience—the spectators too have joined in.
And who is there now to cry 'Author! Author!'?
We believe in our parts. There are no faces behind the masks.
The masks are empty. It's real. *It's real.*

Seventh Elegy

In the Region of Chaos misery is comic,
The Clown is King.
Where everything is grotesque because nothing is understood,
Where the Puer Aeternus is detained by paederasts,
Where there are no correspondences: there is much laughter.
The scale begins on the lowest possible note
And falls back on itself, exhausted.

The blood runs cold in the obscure wood
Where the hoods of the psalliotes are moth-grey in the gloom;
And beyond, against a black sky,
Dying upheavals have reared mountains made of cobwebs.
There a breath is a thousand years.
There words are minerals.
And there it is no longer possible to be led into temptation.

As with a torch whose battery is exhausted,
The light flickers and fades.
In the sunless sky hangs a rainbow made of iron.
The five strings of the lyra are slack and when plucked
Give off a noise like the puff of dust raised by a bullet.
The note hasn't the strength to be born, there are no vibrations,
It crumples and sags like a man shot in the stomach.

The last hour has passed. Now it's too late.
There are only a certain number of chances.
There are only a certain number of opportunities.
Up there, back there, for a time it seemed different
While we were dying. Now it's too late to alter the Past.
Many are called but few are chosen.
And you too will have time to envy the Thief.

'As above, so below.' In my hair the snakes are hissing.
I was blind: I slept: I refused the magical herb
That Hermes offered me. I have condemned my children.
No wonder I cannot bear to look at them.
No wonder children's faces are so full of sadness.
'Oh, I'll leape up to my God, who pulls me doune?'
No one. No one at all. I fell. Nothing, no, no one's to blame.

Now I can join in the laughter. The situation
Isn't tragic any more. To despair, everything's funny.
As there are no correspondences
Nothing has any more meaning.
There's no need to feel embarrassed: Conscience is dead.
Who killed Cock Robin? I did.
With my little arrow, I killed Cock Robin!

The sound travelled, but discovered no opposition.
By the time they met they had grown too far apart.
They were cold, tired, and irritable. Go on,
Go tell the Spartans that we lie here buried for good
Obedient to the Second Law of Thermodynamics.
For here brother may not speak with brother,
Where there is knowledge but no understanding.

Eighth Elegy

FOR LAURA COHN

The Ark rose with the waters, each torrential day,
And floated on the flood.
And what am *I* prepared to do without?
Or is there anything the loss of which
Would make me suicidal?
I am so heavy-laden, so cluttered-up, so rich,
I'm even terrified of distant thunder.

After the rain had stopped their homes were gone.
There was nothing in sight, but the stars were remarkably clear.
All violence had gone out of them and the gentle Dove
Flew from the barque of peace, but failed at first.
Only after three attempts were they proved invulnerable
And the bird came back, dropped a sprig of olive into Noah's lap
And was away, wondering, doubtless to Thisbe.

But how shall I build my ark against the flood
And bear the Green Ear of Wheat to the gentle field?
Rikyū (who knew the value of *one* morning-glory)
Rikyū had built his ark against the flood:
For he who has conquered himself has conquered death,
And he who has conquered death has built his ark
And the rain and the fire and the trampled wheat are one.

The snow melts and the stream runs down to the seed
As a mother to the children she had given up for lost;
And the acorn that is not eaten by swine towers into a tree,
And in the reedy summer gathers the herds into its arms:
And the caterpillar dies into a chrysalis, and after three days
The moth and the butterfly, the night and the day, are reborn
And Jonah was three days in the belly of the whale.

I must die to myself. I am not what I seem.
In the ugliest grub there is perhaps a butterfly.
Sometimes in the face of an orphan I have seen what happens:
For a moment I have understood, and then I've averted my eyes.
I should have stayed and wept, not over Nagasaki,
But over the seed that was left unwatered and withered away:
The end of the world is today and not tomorrow.

In the end when there is nothing remaining;
In the end when there is no more hope;
In the end when there is no longer love;
In the end when there is no one but the child
Who curses God and whimpers continually for his mother;
In the end we'll know if there are any heroes,
If there's anyone who knows how to build an ark.

I have heard a crane calling in the shade.
I am waiting, not daring to breathe, for the young to reply.
I believe! Help thou mine unbelief! When will they answer?
When I break the bowl into fragments ('never again!')
When I seek out and shelter the little boy lost:
When I am unconcerned as the huge firefly:
When I cry welcome to the unsheathed sword: when I can follow
The music of the Ten Strokes of the Wings!

NOTES

FIRST ELEGY

Stanza 3, line 6. A symbol in the Eleusinian Mysteries.
Stanza 5, line 7. The *Ga Grama.*

SECOND ELEGY

Stanza 7, line 4. A reference to a chorus from the *Agamemnon.*
Stanza 7, line 7. The words 'Memory Eternal' are from the Russian
Service from the Dead.

THIRD ELEGY

Stanza 2, line 4. This and the following line are paraphrased from
Goethe.
Stanza 4, line 7. '. . . She had met Lucifer in her visions . . . and she
knew him because he had such hopeless eyes.'
—Maurice Nicoll. *Commentaries.*
Stanza 5, line 7. 'What does your conscience say?—You shall become
who you are.'—Nietzsche.

FOURTH ELEGY

Stanza 1, line 2. Of the Dervishes.
Stanza 2, line 5. Plato.
Stanza 3. c.f. the Yi King, composed by the Emperor Fo-Hi in
3468 B.C.
line 6, c.f. Plato's *Republic* where he refers to the system of
Pythagoras.
Stanza 4, line 7. c.f. Dante, *Paradiso*, 1-103.
Stanza 5 & 6. A paraphrase from the Yo Ki.
Stanza 7, line 6. *La novita del suono e il gran lume di lor cagion mi
accesero un disio mai non sentito di cotanto acume.* . . .

(Paradiso, I, 82.)

FIFTH ELEGY

Stanza 3, line 6. 'I shall hope in the shadow of thy wings until iniquity has passed away.'
—Gregory of Elvira, *Tractatus* II

SIXTH ELEGY

Stanza 2, line 7. In the Greek, Actor = Hypocrite.

Stanza 3, line 1, 'Plutarch tells how Solon, after witnessing an early dramatic performance, rebuked Thespis for encouraging deceit by playacting, and gave warning that before long men would use such methods in earnest; the sage's warning was justified when Peisistratus appeared in the marketplace covered with make-believe wounds and persuaded the people to allot him the bodyguard which he at once used to make himself tyrant.'—D. W. Lucas.

EIGHTH ELEGY

Stanza 3, line 3. The Teamaster Rikyū, to please a guest, sacrificed all his morning-glories to preserve the best. (Suzuki.)

Stanza 7, line 1. An image from the Yi King.

line 6. c.f. the Haiku:

A huge firefly,
Waveringly,
Passes by. (Trans. Dr. Blyth, quoted by Suzuki.)

line 8. The 'Ten Strokes of the Wings' is a Confucian treatise which deals among other things with the trigrams representing and represented by the notes of the scale.